Catholics and Broken Marriage

Catholics and Broken Marriage

John T. Catoir

Ave Maria Press
Notre Dame, Indiana 46556

Library of Congress Catalog Card Number: 78-74434

International Standard Book Number: 0-87793-176-3

© 1979 by Ave Maria Press, Notre Dame, Indiana 46556

Manufactured in the United States of America.

Contents

Introduction

When Father John Reedy called me to do an interview with him for the bimonthly newsletter, *A.D. Correspondence,* I was reluctant. Although I had served as the Chief Judge of the Marriage Tribunal for the Diocese of Paterson for about 10 years, I was no longer a practicing canon lawyer. At the time he called I was the Clergy Personnel Director for the diocese. Nevertheless, he wanted my views on the evolving picture of marriage and divorce in the Catholic church. This little book is an expansion of our conversation. I wanted to offer some encouragement to those who are experiencing the pain of a broken marriage and, at the same time, stand up for the church's right to defend the permanence of the marriage bond.

I have lived and worked through much of the evolution in our marriage tribunals during the past 15 years. When I first took over my diocesan tribunal, it was almost impossible to get an annulment. Cases required proof positive; the grounds for annulment were severely limited, and the tradition was legalistic, not pastoral. I won't bore you with details, but the system often frustrated those judges who felt a pastoral concern for the petitioner.

It took years of struggle on the part of many canonists to convince the American hierarchy that our system was a countersign rather than a sign of salvation. Eventually the bishops agreed that reform was needed and they brought the issue to the pope. Pope Paul VI granted some experimental norms to correct the abuses and these are still in effect at this writing. Enormous changes came about as a result. I will explain them in greater detail in the interview.

I hope the answers I give will be of some help. It isn't easy trying to express in a few words both compassion toward the person in marital difficulty and commitment to the ideal of the permanence of marriage. Our views on these questions may differ. I offer mine, realizing that the authority of the church is to be respected and I submit to that authority in complete peace. We are all bound to implement the law of Jesus Christ.

St. Paul's statement to the Galatians seems to put the whole thing in perspective. "Help carry one another's burdens; in that way you will fulfill the law of Jesus Christ." Ever since I read that line, I have understood clearly that the defense of principles must be done within the context of love. There is only one law: the law of charity. The challenge is to live that law as best you can. St. Augustine offered some sage advice along these lines. "Do what you can do, and pray for what you cannot yet do."

— Fr. John Catoir

1. The Extent of the Problem

How rapidly is the divorce rate rising?

Well, the *New York Times* published some statistics ("The Family in Transition," November 27, 1977) which indicated:

- The divorce rate has doubled in the last 10 years.

- Two out of every five children born in this decade will live in a single-parent home for at least part of their youth.

- The number of households headed by women has increased by more than a third in this decade, and more than doubled in one generation.

- More than half of all mothers with school-age children

11

now work outside the home, as do more than a third of mothers with children under the age of three.

- One out of every three schoolchildren lives in a home headed by only one parent or relative.

- Day care of irregular quality is replacing the parental role in many working families, and there has been extraordinary growth in the classifications that sociologists call "latchkey children," i.e., children unsupervised for portions of the day, usually between the end of school and the parents' return from work.

- The average number of children per family has dropped from a recent high of 3.8 in 1957 to 2.04 today, which means natural families are decreasing, while legal kinships through divorce and remarriage are expanding.

How do you interpret all this?

It's hard to say. Some sophisticated sociologists differ widely on the meaning of it all, so I won't pretend to interpret it correctly, but there's one thing involved for certain—the children of these marriages suffer. Many children have the resiliency to adjust to the trauma of a broken home but many more do not. The results are far-reaching. It's difficult to estimate the overall effect this will have on the character of the American people in the long run, because divorce is a breeding ground for emotional sickness.

Isn't this happening the same way all over the world?

Yes. In the major industrial nations the rising divorce rate is a common phenomenon. That doesn't mean it's normal. Widespread mistrust and emotional pain can only lead to a lessening of the will to love. Unless we all grow in our capacity to love we will make the world a living hell. For some it's that already, isn't it?

Part of the statistics cited mentioned the rise in the number of working mothers. How do you assess that?

Mothers are going back to work for a variety of reasons. Family finances account for most of it, especially in the lower- and middle-income groups. The increase of inflationary pressure doesn't help much. The women usually try to augment their family income. They work for a specific goal: to buy a car or put a child through school. However, more and more women are telling us that they cannot adjust to the boredom of housework. Many of them use the word "trapped" to explain their feelings about homemaking and child-rearing. They go to work to escape the discomfort of their routine, but sometimes the remedy turns out to be worse than the disease.

What do you mean?

Well, it often happens that, instead of relieving her "trapped feelings," she becomes trapped in a new situation. She exchanges the role of housewife for the trap of eight hours behind a typewriter. Eight hours a day is a long work period for a woman who has children and who must return to meet their needs in the evening. Now let me be fair. I know some women must work, and they are heroic in their efforts to support and raise a family, but many women have taken jobs when they did not have to. All they needed were some mental stimulation and legitimate diversion.

Do you take issue with working mothers?

No, not really. As I said, many women have to work and I respect them very much. There are more saints among these working mothers than anyone knows. I do take issue, however, with the liberationists who sarcastically ridicule mothers who devote themselves to home and children as though it was demeaning to womanhood. It's becoming more and more clear, as statistics come in, that child-rearing ideally is a full-time job. Day-care programs and schools cannot supply the love and concern needed by children as they grow up. However, when a working parent communicates love, children are often capable of an extraordinary amount of self-sacrifice. In those cases the child's character is actually strengthened. I just pray for the working mother. It isn't easy.

I'd like to say something else before you go on. I'd like to remind the divorcees who might read these words that I do not judge them, nor do I think anyone else should judge them. Every situation is different and many times I have advised people to get a divorce. Sometimes a person has a moral obligation to divorce.

But I hope the reader will understand that there are two different groups who will read these words: the married and the divorced. I am so conscious of the millions of marriages just struggling along that I cannot forget the impact my words might have. I want to be sympathetic and supportive to the divorcee, but I also want to defend the rights of children to grow up with both parents in one family. While defending the permanence of marriage and demanding greater sacrifice from the parents who are still together, I want to treat the divorcee with respect. Many divorcees are innocent victims of a great tragedy and they need help and understanding. I hope they will understand my intent.

What if the parent has no choice but to work?

Then there is no choice and the parent should try very hard to compensate with the quality of time given to make up for the reduced quantity of time. A sincere and loving parent will be able to communicate love and, for a faith-filled person, there is always grace. God's grace can supply what may be lacking in a particular family structure. But when conditions are normal, and a mother does not have to work, it is clearly in the best interests of the children—especially if they are little—and probably in her own best interests, that she stay out of the job market. Why do some women equate growth and personal fulfillment with getting a paycheck at the end of the week? The price they pay is often more demeaning than enhancing to their person.

How do you think your views square with others?

Well, there was a survey by CBS News and the *New York Times* on this in October of 1977. Overall, 54% of those interviewed said, "Yes, a woman should work even if she has a husband capable of supporting her." This 54% needs to be broken down. Among those between the ages of 18 to 29, 75% answered yes. Of those between the ages of 30 and 44, 57% answered yes. It seems the older the sample group, the smaller the percentage. Those over 65 had only 24% answering yes to the same question. One interesting note came out of the survey: 60% balked at the idea of uprooting a family in which both parents work in order to allow the woman to accept a promotion in another part of the country, with 11% in favor of the move and 14% holding that it would depend on the circumstances in each case.

What do the surveys show on the question of the actual cause of divorce? For instance, outside pressures? money problems?

A popular belief seems to be that the pressures of the modern world are behind the divorce increase. Surprisingly, those surveyed dismissed, by a two to one ratio, the idea that outside pressures had contributed to the nation's rising divorce rate. Instead, they tended to blame couples for "not trying hard enough to stay together." Very interesting, isn't it?

Yes, it is. What do you think gives rise to this idea?

I don't know for sure, but I think a number of people who have experienced a divorce close to them have a strong opinion that the couple gave up too soon. The children of broken marriages want the marriage to stay together, even if it isn't perfect harmony all the time. The parents of the divorcing couple and their friends also want the couple to try harder. In fact, they would like them to stop thinking of themselves and think of the damage their decision will inflict on all those around them.

Is this really fair? I mean, who can tell a couple how much pain they must endure?

I don't mean to make light of the pain. What I'm trying to say is that the survey dismissed outside pressures as the main cause of the rising divorce rate by a two to one ratio, and I think I understand why. Of course the pressures of the modern world are more intense than in former generations, and this has a decided bearing on the way people behave. But I think there is a widespread epidemic abroad which renders many modern people unwilling, or unable, to endure hardship and pain for any length of time. The meaning of sacrifice has changed and therefore its value is more quickly disdained.

Years ago the idea of divorce was unthinkable, and many men confidently abused their women because society's pressure virtually empowered them to do so. Some women, of course, were able to do the same thing in reverse by their personal powers. In either case I can see the dangers of forcing people to stay together in hostile circumstances, but I agree wholeheartedly with the survey, which placed the main blame on the parties themselves; too many of them simply do not try hard enough. If they knew the terrible wound that divorce inflicts on the children, they would put forth greater effort to make the marriage work.

But many of them try heroically to save the marriage, and nothing works.

That's true. The question is not a simple one to deal with. I'm very much aware that it takes two to achieve the ideal of permanence in marriage. If one party is determined to destroy the marriage, the other party is helpless. Very often the children do not comprehend the delicacy of the interaction between parents, and they sometimes blame the wrong one. Subtle injustices and sometimes brazen injustices exist which are intolerable for any morally upright person. My mind, however, cannot shake free of the injustice done to the children by parents who selfishly put themselves first. Husbands and wives, for instance, who consider infidelity only a minor indiscretion. They become emotionally involved with another and grow to despise the marriage which only impinges on their claim to freedom. What a cruel blow to a spouse who has given trust and love, and what an injustice to the children to create a smoke screen of constant arguing to disguise the real cause of the breakup — marital infidelity.

On the one hand you admit the right to divorce and on the other you seem to speak against it.

I find it impossible to do otherwise. Of course, some people must divorce. But it's too easy to make excuses, blaming the wrong person for the wrong reasons. I see at a basic level that the problem involves a loss of spiritual values in our day. It isn't always a question of not trying hard enough; it is more a matter of knowing what the basic ground rules for survival are all about. So many people simply do not know. Many of them have been spoiled. Their own satisfaction is of supreme importance to them, their first priority. Even people who believe themselves to be religious have demonstrated their fundamental egoism.

Isn't that just a bit too judgmental?

Each one has to be the judge of his own behavior. I do not judge any individual. I am concerned with the hypocrisy of the day. God is not in the place of highest honor. Doing what God wants is of little importance to many people, even some who profess to be religious. Individualistic thinking will usually subvert a relationship.

What do you mean?

Well, suppose you bought a brand-new car. With it came the manufacturer's manual telling you how to maintain and care for your new possession. If you threw the manual away and ignored the ground rules of maintenance, forgetting to add oil and lubrication, it would only be a short time before a serious breakdown would occur. Human life is like that. We are made by God, and we need to follow the manufacturer's manual. Life needs religion and moral integrity. Without it the flow of happiness and health can be seriously disrupted. To neglect your spiritual needs is the worst thing you can do. Our people have to pray more, call upon God's grace more, if they are to overcome the obstacles they face.

In your judgment, much of the problem of the increasing divorce rate is related to the neglect of spiritual values in one or both of the parties to a divorce?

That's right. I think it begins in the heart of the individual.

How do you account for the fact that many atheists have good marriages?

There are many secularists and even atheists who make their marriages work, and they do it precisely because they have agreed upon a lifestyle which is essentially in harmony with what we know to be the path of righteous living. Fidelity, love, patience, sincerity . . . all these virtues can exist in so-called atheists. They may not see the religious aspect of their lifestyle, but they have exercised good sense, and they have the natural virtue which is essential for a reasonably happy life. When you bring children into the world, you owe them care and devotion. Needless risks are very unwise. A lot of people see this clearly without the need of religion, but the major religions of the world all foster these values. To ignore them is folly.

I know you believe that other factors are involved which contribute to the escalating divorce rate. Can we discuss them for a while?

Yes. I want to make it clear that my interest in helping people survive the experience of divorce is not based on a casual attitude toward divorce itself. I want to help people find peace of mind as they pick up the pieces, but I think they will easily make the same mistakes over again if they do not identify and correct their real problem.

What, then, do you think are the other causes which contribute to the increase in divorce?

The next two causes, I believe, would be the increasing materialistic pace of modern life, and our own failure to teach children how to become good husbands and wives.

Now that's interesting—not preparing the children properly. Do you think a lot of adults are not really ready when they get married?

Some of them are not really adults. In addition to knowing little or nothing about the laws of survival, which I consider the moral law to be, they do not have any real grounding in common sense. There are also a lot of skills that must be learned when one marries, and it's extremely difficult to begin this all at once. The problem is compounded when you have two babes in the woods trying to grow up overnight. It just doesn't happen in a day. You can't plant an acorn in the morning and expect that afternoon to sit in the shade of an oak.

Could you explain that further?

I remember a quote by Ashley Montagu back in the late 60s. He was the chairman of the Anthropology Department at Rutgers University. "Most people become parents without any qualifications whatsoever." He continued in this vein, claiming that most people in our culture don't know anything about love and can't communicate it to their offspring or instill in them a love of fellow man. His words were biting, "The American family is an institution for the production of mental illness in each of its members, and what's being produced is a generation of monomaniacal egomaniacs who must succeed at all costs. . . . They're dead to everything human."

His criticism is a bit overstated for my taste, but he makes a good point. We have a real problem in this country, not only because of the communication gap between the generations, but because we have developed a precarious system of marriage which is based on romantic love. We encourage freedom of choice in the selection of one's spouse. Now this is humane and the opposite may be unthinkable, but in more than half the world, even this very day, the independent right to select one's spouse is not given to the young, precisely because their judgment is not regarded as mature enough for so important a decision.

In many cultures a woman is told whom she will marry and it is immaterial if she feels attraction or even love for her selected mate. She is assured that love follows the second child. Countless millions of women over the centuries have followed the advice of their elders and their success in marriage is statistically far superior to our own. Today the children shift for themselves and we are witnessing the results.

But surely free choice has been supported for 200 years in this country, and only recently have we witnessed the outbreak of divorce.

It has not being going on universally, and not for 200 years. There have been much more stringent controls over the choice allowed children than we have today, even though the freedom of choice was essentially their own. But suppose, for argument's sake, that full freedom was there for 200 years. Marriage based on romantic love was unheard of in most countries of the world until rather recent times.

Why do you mention this in connection with our failure to prepare kids for marriage?

Because we underestimate the tremendous burden placed upon the shoulders of our young people. In their immaturity, at a time when they have not even begun to understand or even become accustomed to their own sexuality, they are "falling in love," and being drawn into making the most important decision of their lives. You don't really understand our young people unless you grasp the depth of their fears. They have witnessed all this failure at love. They have been victimized by their parents' mistakes, and they have grown very suspicious of romantic love. They postpone marriage, refuse to make commitments; they enter into common-law unions and stand against the older generation's value system because they see it doesn't work. They know they have to be careful, but they don't know how.

The mystery of transitory romantic emotions baffles even the most experienced people. The young, who are the most susceptible of all to emotional upheavals, have a particularly difficult time experimenting with life, acting as though nothing from the wisdom of the past can be trusted.

There's no going back to the arranged marriage. Let's face it. Life is trial and error. We have to face that fact and do the best we can.

It is true that one really learns about life by living it, and I don't suggest going back. Trial and error is the greatest teacher. But young people have a great capacity for learning more. We have not developed a method of exposing them to the vast amount of new knowledge which we possess in the field of personal interaction, human communication, psychology, homemaking and child-rearing.

The first great need is to help young people to develop

an understanding of themselves, so that they may more readily accept themselves. With self-acceptance comes the base necessary for personal growth. If individuals enter marriage without self-acceptance they will soon fail to love their spouse.

This is basically a communication problem, isn't it?

Yes, it is. There is a whole range of communications problems which prevent the ordinary young couple from enjoying its full share of happiness in marriage. I have seen so many beautiful young people come before me in misery over their marriage problems, so many who started out with a bright and shiny future, only to see it all crumble in a short time before their very eyes. They received good schooling, good health care, and the like, but something was missing. They lacked the personal strength needed to love well. They didn't know how to love, or they chose a mate who lacked the capacity to love.

The most important thing that parents can do for their children is to teach them how to love. It's not an easy matter, but it must be done. The church should be involved in helping parents to teach their children about love. The first school is the home, and spiritual values must be taught there. But steps should be taken by the church to develop something substantial and meaningful in educating the young about marriage. All that canon law requires for marriage is that the local pastor give a set of six instructions.

What do you suggest?

I believe we have to prepare kids for the challenge of adult life early in their training. Both public and parochial schools have failed them. When the time for marriage comes upon them, very few pastors or assistant pastors can give an adequate premarital preparation in the short time available, because of their own inexperience in the field of marriage and their limited knowledge of the persons involved. Besides, the seeds of failure may have been sown in these persons' very choice of each other as partners in marriage. The pastor has no real way of knowing this unless he is unusually intuitive, and even then, it is not his place to block the plans and dreams of young lovers.

What we need is a preparation in depth, an ongoing preparation, beginning in grammar school and continuing throughout the remainder of the student's formal education. This is a much bigger problem than sex education. Courses should be introduced to our school systems, both public and parochial, which are designed to educate children in the fundamental values of life relating to the attainment of a happy love relationship.

A knowledge of the difference between male and female psychology is something that should be taught in high school and should not be left to the agonizing trial and error process of ordinary human experience. Untold misery could be avoided if a young man had a fundamental grasp of the basic needs and frustrations of his sexual counterpart. And the girl should come to understand the motives and reasoning of the male.

Young people should be given a thorough understanding not only of the opposite sex but of themselves as well. The problem of self-understanding and self-acceptance should be openly confronted and gradually resolved, before young people even consider marriage.

You mentioned sex education. Could you go into that a little?

Sex instruction is an important concern in the whole process of achieving harmony between the sexes, but it can be overestimated. Marriage is a much more vast experience than sex, just as love is a much more vast experience than marriage. Nevertheless, all are intimately related within the framework of a wholesome life. The unpredictability of sex is a matter of common experience. The pain and suffering of an unhappy love is the subject matter of thousands of songs. The interaction of lovers is extremely personal, but it can be explored in a scientific way, not for the purpose of imposing prohibitions but to enlighten youngsters so that they can be more firmly based when they choose a partner. Their powers of understanding can be developed and needless suffering can be avoided. It is true that once the heart seizes upon its beloved there is not much anyone can do to educate a person, but much can be done before that time comes.

What are some of the other reasons why marriage failures are more prevalent today?

There are sociological reasons. What I mentioned before pertained to the individual's personal life. When a counselor tries to help a couple having marriage difficulties, he or she should first try to identify each of the problems: which problems arise out of the personality inadequacies of the two parties, or out of their inability to interrelate; which problems are thrust upon them by outside forces. When I speak of sociological factors, I'm talking about the pressures of the world.

For instance?

Well, the fast pace of living. The ever-increasing mobility required of families. Years ago, only military personnel and a few others were subject to a constant moving around. Now nearly every man who works for a large corporation, in order to be advanced, must be willing to move lock, stock and barrel, wife and family, when the company dictates.

Another reason for the rise in the divorce rate involves the abdication of family responsibilities. Once upon a time a family unit provided its own life support system. Everything from health care to recreation was done at home. Now everything, or nearly everything, is done outside the home. School, work, sports activities, socializing, even many meals are eaten away from the home. It is estimated that one-fourth of the meals eaten in America are eaten in restaurants. In 10 years that figure is expected to rise to 40 percent.

So it isn't hard to figure out that the pressures pulling the family apart are enormous.

Right. With everyone moving in a different direction, no one has time for listening, understanding and, in many cases, loving.

You didn't mention the moral climate in which we live. This is certainly a factor, isn't it?

I didn't forget it. The moral atmosphere has deteriorated to the point that sexual promiscuity and infidelity are considered normal. The traveling husband is subject to severe pressures and temptations and, to a lesser degree, so is the wife. The children, especially the teenagers, grow up believing that sex is a game, a form of recreation.

It isn't until reality fully hits that people come to see the terrible pain and misery caused by the failure to control one's sexuality. Those sad love songs we hear are ample evidence of that.

Many people I know come to marriage without much in the way of practical living skills. I don't think this causes divorce, but it can help to sour a marriage if other things are going wrong as well.

I know what you mean. Apart from these matters of the heart there is the whole question of developing the tools of a happy marriage relationship. Managing money, developing the will to bear discomfort, learning to cope with the problem of boredom, and delegating various responsibilities according to the respective talents of the husband and wife are means to successful sharing that can be learned. And in more general terms, learning about the psychology of man and woman would go a long way toward preparing young people for problems before they descend full force. There really should be a reservoir of knowledge and understanding built up within us as we grow up.

How does psychology fit into this?

The ability to love can be nurtured by an awareness of the motives and the actions of others. A great deal could be done in this regard to help youngsters realize their potential for giving, and release them from inordinate fear about the future.

Education, it is true, is not a panacea for all our marriage problems. But the basic education we are discussing is the kind that comes from experience— experience with parents who love each other and relatives who care for one another. This firm basis in love, backed by school training in mental health, would provide material that could make a substantial difference in the lives of many people. It would simply be a matter of refocusing our attention from the peripheral idea of success to the central meaning of life, namely, the joy and blessing of real love. We ought not rest until we provide a better preparation for marriage.

Name a few key ideas you think important in preparing kids for marriage.

The first conclusion is obvious: Beware of overinflated expectations. The high expectations that Americans place on marriage as a means to personal growth, intimacy, nonpossessive caring and sexual fulfillment cannot be realistically met. The social and psychological milieu of American life creates extraordinary stress on family life. In America today a young couple needs greater maturity, greater moral character and a stronger commitment to maintain a successful marriage than was necessary in earlier generations, or is necessary today in less industrialized societies. Young people are fully aware of that and they are making all kinds of adjustments to compensate, but they need our help. We live in a society which pressures young people into irresponsible decision-making. Many more invalid marriages result and the church is trying to face up to this by expanding its annulment services.

How many young Americans do you think are actually capable of entering into and sustaining the burdens and obligations of marriage?

No one can know that, but I wonder if we should be presuming that all of their marriages are valid? So much evidence seems to point to the fact that they lack the maturity and moral resolve to make their marriages work. We have to be there to prepare them better, but if they fail we also have to be there to help them pick up the pieces. Some divorcees are victims of circumstances beyond their control. Some of them are saints. I am grateful that the Holy Spirit has led many churchmen to reach out and help these people in the growing ministry to the divorced. Generally speaking, the official church has been encouraging to these initiatives. We thank God for helping us to grow in our understanding of these difficult human problems.

2. The Annulment Process

Could you describe some of the broad changes that have occurred in the handling of marriage cases in the past decade? We keep hearing about developments in this area.

I would say that before 1960 the record shows that tribunal efficiency was at a low level. Very few cases got through because of strong resistance to granting annulments. Strict application of the law was the norm and there were elaborate requirements in terms of evidence and legal procedure. Only the perfect cases seemed able to get through the tribunals, if the cases were heard at all. Most tribunals, outside of the largest cities, handled only one or two formal annulments a year. The largest cities like New York or Los Angeles might have given judgments on 25 cases or so. More than that would have been an outstanding accomplishment.

31

Aren't procedures in these cases similar to the procedures of a civil court? Evidence is submitted, canon lawyers are consulted . . . ?

In general outline that would be true, and it is certainly one's first impression upon viewing the system. The court does operate according to a set of procedures that are strictly enumerated in Book Four of the Code of Canon Law, *De Processibus*. That section describes the procedures for all judicial hearings within the church, including marriage cases. In contrast with civil law, marriage cases are decided not by jury but by a panel of three judges. A canon lawyer acts as Defender of the Bond, a sort of devil's advocate who argues the case in favor of the bond of marriage. There is also another attorney, the Procurator Advocate, who argues for the petitioner.

And there have been developments in the efficiency of this system in the past few years?

Yes. There were pressures that provoked changes. Mainly, I believe, the pressure came from priests involved in the court system who were trying, as human beings, to help people, but were hamstrung by the law. They took steps to alter the ineffective and merciless aspects of the application of the law, but they did not attempt to change the law itself, insofar as it is faithful to the Gospel teaching of Christ on indissolubility. The effort to deal with human needs in a pastoral way required a new approach to the application of the law. This was not always possible before 1960.

Then around May of 1968, a special committee of the Canon Law Society began to review the problem with the idea of reconsidering the effectiveness of the procedural laws. They developed a set of 27 norms for reform, and these were accepted at the annual convention of the Canon Law Society in September of 1968. Then the recommendations were sent to the American bishops who deliberated on them. In their meeting of April, 1969, after making a few minor changes, the bishops voted to forward the norms to Rome to see if the Holy See would approve them. Rome made a few alterations and we received experimental permission for 23 reforms in July of 1970.

These had to do mainly with matters of procedure?

Yes, they covered such issues as which tribunal is competent to hear a specific case; or what should be the number of judges necessary for a specific case. For instance, tribunals which were short-staffed and had a backlog of cases were allowed to assign one judge to hear the case instead of the panel of three. This was an important breakthrough and it made for much greater efficiency. But for me, the most important breakthrough was the ruling that the Defender of the Bond was not required to appeal the case to a court of second instance if he felt that the case was compelling in its argumentation. Previously, the annulment could only be granted after there were two concurring affirmative judgments. If you received an affirmative judgment in the first court, you had to get a second affirmative in the court of appeals. If the second decision was negative, the case would be appealed to the Roman Rota, which served as the court of third instance and dealt with the most difficult cases.

And this might take five or six years?

Easily. Sometimes 10. Some cases took 20 years.
The new norms were approved as a three-year experiment,
beginning in July of 1970. Fortunately, they have been
extended. However, they apply only to the United States,
and this has created a certain amount of tension with other
countries concerned about reforming their own procedures.

**I gather that another major development involves the
increase in the grounds allowed for the invalidation of a
marriage.**

That's correct; this is a reform in the substantive law,
the grounds for nullity. What lies behind this development is
the present-day explosion of knowledge — new knowledge
in the fields of psychiatry, sociology and human behavior.
This knowledge has given canon lawyers a new viewpoint on
marriage, which previously may have been understood
simply as a legal contract. It may surprise some to know
that much of the new thinking came from jurists in Rome:
from the Roman Rota or the Vicariate Appeal Court (the
court that handles second-appeal cases from the dioceses of
Italy). Specific decisions coming from Rome opened our
eyes to new possibilities.

Could you give an example of such a case?

Yes. A case was recorded in the *Monitor Ecclesiasticus,*
Volume Two, for 1968. It appeared in the Vicariate Appeal
Court of Rome and the decision was rendered by Father
Mark Said, granting an annulment on the basis of
immaturity. Canon 1082 states that matrimonial consent
cannot be validly given unless the contracting parties know
at least that marriage is a permanent union between man
and woman for the procreation of children. Father Said

raised the question: What kind of knowledge is required?
He suggested that the essential knowledge must be
appreciative knowledge, not merely conceptual knowledge.
In other words, the person "must have sufficient discretion
and maturity of judgment in order to give deliberate
matrimonial consent."

**Obviously, this idea must open the door to a whole new area
of inquiry in marriage cases.**

Yes, it does. Some dioceses are not using immaturity
as grounds for annulment because it is such a broad and
novel idea. But we shouldn't be afraid of it. If such
annulments are being granted in Rome on solid canonical
grounds, we shouldn't pose an overly strict interpretation.
We shouldn't be more strict than Rome. The fact is,
annulments are being validly granted because a person
didn't have maturity of judgment at the time of the marriage.

**Isn't it true that many young people do not appear to
appreciate the permanence of marriage? The priest asks
them if they intend their marriage to be a permanent union
and they reply, "I guess so." In terms of this new norm,
would many of these marriages be regarded canonically as
invalid?**

The presumption is for validity in every case, but the
question you raise has an obvious relevance. Trying to
estimate the level of maturity in individuals at the time of
their marriage is not easy, but it seems true that many
marriages today would not stand up under canonical
scrutiny. Also, immaturity is a broad and dangerous word,
because everybody is immature to some extent. It's a relative
term.

This decision was reported in 1968. I would assume that a good many dioceses have used the norm.

Yes, they have.

And the record shows a fair number of dissolutions of marriages on this basis?

Yes, and there is a similar category used by the Rota to grant annulments. Canonically, it is known as "lack of conjugal love." Lack of conjugal love is a consideration that could really open the floodgates. I suppose it could be assumed that any marriage which failed lacked conjugal love. But it has a much more strict application in the court. I would refer to a Canadian theologian, Father Germain Lesage, OMI, writing in *Studia Canonica* of 1972. He proposed 15 concrete elements which are essential to a community of conjugal love. If these were lacking to a vital degree at the time of marriage, then the marriage would not be canonically valid.

Would you name a few?

Yes. For instance, to be a valid marriage the union must have "oblatory love," that is, a love which is not aimed at egoistic satisfaction of oneself but which goes out to provide for the welfare and happiness of the partner. There must also be "respect for conjugal morality and for the partner's conscience in sexual relations." Someone who had only a manipulative attitude in sexual relations with the partner would be depriving the partner of an essential marriage right, i.e., the right to a natural sexual relationship. Another essential element is "respective responsibility of both husband and wife in providing for the material welfare of the home, stability in work, budgetary foresight."

That sounds like immaturity in relation to money matters.

It's that, certainly, but it relates more to the will to provide. We run into cases where the men actually have no interest in providing for the material well-being of their families. The wife is constantly plagued with the hardships that accrue from his refusal either to work or to bring home his earnings. It gradually becomes an intolerable situation. This is an abnormality, of course, but in times past the tribunal would simply not handle such cases. The old bromide, you made your bed now sleep in it, was usually the rule.

What other actions would imply a lack of the degree of responsibility considered essential for marriage?

One thing considered necessary for true consent is a "moral and psychological responsibility in the mastery of irrational passions, impulses or instincts." The absence of this would endanger harmony and order in the marriage. For example, take the person who is psychologically incapable of marital fidelity and becomes a constant embarrassment to the spouse. Assume that this is not a simple question of human weakness. The person is not only a chronic violator of marital fidelity, but flaunts it. This gives rise to the belief that the person is incapable psychologically of making a commitment to any relationship which requires trust and fidelity. He or she would be psychologically incapable of a true marriage relationship. As you can see, all these norms point to some psychological flaw or personality disorder. This has more to do with the capacity of a person to give true consent than with the act of consent itself.

How would you determine whether such a disorder is present?

In the beginning we used to place heavy emphasis on the testimony of psychiatrists who could give an expert diagnosis of the person's trouble. This was one way of ascertaining whether the person had the capacity to sustain the burdens of marriage. But these psychological reports are not always necessary. We do not always need a professional evaluation when there is an obvious pattern, such as constant infidelity, from the beginning. This might persuade a judge either that the necessary level of conjugal love is lacking in the marriage, or that one of the partners has a personality disorder and therefore lacks the capacity to enter into the contract in the first place.

Assume that your investigation reveals the lack of such a necessary attitude, or some incapacity such as you have described. You are probably making the determination not only that this person was incapable of entering into a valid marriage in the past, but also that he is probably incapable of doing so in the future, unless a change in the pattern of his or her behavior occurs.

That's right. We don't like to lay down laws about the future, because we hope that lessons can be learned from past mistakes. We believe that growth is possible. Occasionally we put a *monitum* on the decision. In other words, we notify the proper chancery office that before this person can enter into another Catholic marriage the tribunal should be contacted.

And the tribunal might advise the parish that, even though the person may be canonically free to marry, his psychological state might still render him incapable of entering into a valid marriage.

We would recommend some form of psychological help, to determine the person's present state.

You mentioned earlier that some diocesan courts recognize these norms of character disorder and others do not. Let's assume that a person's marriage broke up because of such a disorder, but he or she lives in a diocese that does not recognize this as sufficient grounds for annulment. What can be done?

One alternative is to apply to a diocese which does. Under the new norms, you can apply for permission to bring your case before a tribunal other than the diocese of your residence or the diocese where the marriage took place. It may mean extensive correspondence and several trips to another city, but you do not have to change your place of residence to apply to another diocese.

Suppose a man applied for an annulment some years ago and received a negative judgment. Later he marries outside the church. He reads this and realizes that this new ruling has a bearing on his situation. Should he resubmit his case?

That would be the ideal. However, one could well understand the pain involved. The person has already suffered one rejection. He could have considerable apprehension about undergoing the judicial process all over again. Yet, it is certainly possible for the case to be resubmitted.

I think such people who cannot go through it all again ought to have the courage of their convictions. In every case that I have dealt with on the basis of conscience or, as we call it, the internal forum, the discussion of the case revealed to me that the person had no sense or awareness of sin in the second marriage. The only problem was that the church did not recognize the marriage. I try to help these people understand that even if the church hasn't acknowledged what they in their hearts seem to know to be the truth, that does not deprive them of union with Christ. In other words, there might be a canonical problem in their relation with the church, but not necessarily a moral problem in their relation with God.

As a priest, it seems to me that we should be building bridges here, doing everything in our power to mend what may have been unjustly broken. Fortunately, the penalty of excommunication has been lifted, but I should note that you can't receive such a penalty in the church anyway unless you have committed a serious sin. These people, in their conscience, have not committed sins; in fact, some have even been heroic in virtue in their determination to make an intolerable marriage work.

This brings up another problem. Formerly a social stigma was attached to living in a marriage not recognized by the church. There were social pressures to get a case like that resolved. But there is little if any stigma attached to it now. Only a person in good conscience would bother to come to the church court.

Correct. Only serious, well-intentioned people come in. Those who don't care about their relationship with the church never come back. We usually see those who really care about their union with God and, for the most part, their actions show that God's grace is active in them. Of course, there are some who come only because they hope to marry a good Catholic.

What about a case like this, known to me personally — a man's marriage breaks up after several years. He takes the case to his marriage court, giving as testimony his word that there was a defect in the marriage regarding nonconsummation. He isn't able to establish this fact to the satisfaction of the tribunal because there are no other witnesses. For the rest of his life this man lives a single life. Yet he had no reason to lie, and had no reason — other than his conscience — for living the life he now lives. Isn't there some injustice being done here?

Yes. Humanly speaking, this man has suffered a great burden as a result of our canonical discipline, and his case should have been tried on other grounds. Of course, the church is not wrong in asking for proof in cases of nonconsummation. Sometimes one party claims nonconsummation and the other party denies it. Either way, all these nonconsummation cases are sent to Rome, because they are not annulments but dissolutions.

Frankly, I think this procedure regarding nonconsummation is appalling. It is very hard to prove, and most cases where nonconsummation is the issue can be argued on other grounds. Clearly, if a marriage was never consummated there are other serious defects in the relationship — perhaps a psychological disorder or some kind of impotence. The case can be tried on other grounds, without the need for such strict proofs of nonconsummation.

What do you mean when you say nonconsummation cases are not annulments?

Just that. In an annulment the church declares that the marriage never validly existed. It's a declaration that the marriage was a legal fiction. In the case of a nonconsummated marriage, the church recognizes it as a legal contract witnessed by a priest and two other witnesses; and in the case of a baptized person, the church recognizes it as a sacrament. But because the consent was never ratified through bodily union, the church is willing to dissolve the marriage. This is really a Catholic divorce. The pope grants the dissolution based on the fact of nonconsummation and the parties are free to remarry. Of course, if one party is the sole cause of the problem, that person would not be allowed to marry again in the church as long as the problem was not corrected.

If a marriage is supposed to be indissoluble how can the church grant any annulments or dissolutions?

It is true that marriage is indissoluble, but it is also true that in order to have indissolubility you must first have a marriage. The court tries to determine this. Let me explain the law on this.

The marriage contract is more than the juridical consent of two grown people of the opposite sex. The sacrament of matrimony is the consecration of human love.

It is a contract, the consecration of a mutual commitment. Society regards it as an authentic expression of the human will to love. For Catholics the marriage contract is itself the sacrament. The two parties confer it upon each other; the priest is merely a qualified witness.

The matter and form of this sacrament is expressed in the mutual giving and receiving of all that marriage means in terms of human love, namely, care, responsibility, respect, fidelity and sexual union. The sacrament is the consecration of human love.

As I've already noted, in an annulment the church formally recognizes that an essential element of sacramental marriage was missing. Thus, according to its understanding of the sacramental reality, the union never existed.

In a dissolution, the situation is more complicated. Some of the elements are recognized. For example, the exchange of consent before an authorized priest and witnesses. But if the fullness of the relationship has never been achieved (for some reason the marriage was never consummated) the church can, by formal action, withdraw the witness it has given in the ceremony.

When there has been no essential defect, and the fullness of commitment has been given by responsible Christians, the church teaches that marriage is indissoluble, that it establishes a permanent commitment before God which cannot be dissolved by any authority, civil or ecclesiastical.

What does the canon law have to say about the purpose of marriage?

According to Canon 1082, par. 1: "Marriage is a permanent society between a man and a woman for the purpose of procreating children." The Second Vatican Council further refined church teaching by emphasizing the importance of mutual love of the partners and the necessity for this love to develop and mature.

Of course, we know a marriage is permanent as long as it does not break up. Some marriages, in spite of the indissoluble character of matrimony, fall by their own weight for any number of reasons. One of the most common reasons is that one or both parties, at the time of the marriage, were actually unable to give or receive unselfish human love. The courtship seems to have been a delusion wherein one or both parties became infatuated with their own immature romantic emotions.

A lot of marriages fail for that reason, but what about some of the more bizarre cases? I understand that the church never used to give annulments for cases such as known homosexuality.

That's true. It's hard to believe. There are rare instances, no doubt, of inverts who have deeply loved their spouses, but there are more instances of homosexuals who use their spouse merely as a cover for their clandestine activity. Only recently has there been any hope for an annulment on these grounds. Very few tribunals in the world would accept such a case in the past. Why? Not only because these cases are almost impossible to prove, but because the law taken strictly did not enable the tribunal to process the case. Only by expanding and developing legal concepts can such a case be brought forward for consideration. This is already being done by the more advanced and better staffed tribunals, and it is becoming more common because of a new emphasis on the necessary subjective capacity of each individual to sustain the marriage. This is a shift in the investigation's emphasis from the efficient cause to the material cause of the sacrament.

What do you mean by that?

An examination of the nature of Christian marriage can help to explain the basis for this line of reasoning. Marriage is traditionally viewed under two aspects: marriage *in fieri* and marriage *in facto esse*. Marriage *in fieri* considers the man and the woman as consenting subjects, as the efficient cause of the contract. Traditionally, the main emphasis for determining validity has been on the quality of consent given on the day of the wedding. It is in the area of defective consent that most annulments had been granted in the past. Such a heavily restricting legal approach to human failures in marriage neglected to take into consideration wider possibilities.

The church has also viewed marriage *in facto esse,* as a state of life. In this view, man and woman are considered the material cause of the sacrament. Here we keep in mind the social aspect of the sacrament, namely, the community's recognition of this couple as officially joined together in a stable way of life. The community gives witness to the external consent, and in this sense the priest acts as a qualified witness for the community. The community on this basis accepts the couple as married.

The community aspect, however, has nothing to do with the actual conferring of the sacrament. It is the mutual exchange of the love commitment that constitutes the matter and form of the sacrament. In this view, validity depends on the radical fitness or ability of the two parties to love, to enter into and sustain a marriage union. When the capacity to accept and carry the obligations of married life comes into prominence as a requisite for the sacrament, there is much hope for a more human approach in solving marital difficulties.

In other words, the homosexual is really not material for a heterosexual marriage?

Exactly!

Well, that's pretty obvious, isn't it? I mean, why go into such an elaborate explanation?

Well, it may be obvious to you but, believe it or not, the church refused to touch these cases for centuries, believing that homosexuality was always a sin to be overcome, and never a condition or state. I think most people believed this, down through the centuries. This view is not psychologically acceptable today. The reason I went into the elaborate explanation was to flesh out what I was saying earlier about the lack of maturity or lack of conjugal love as grounds for nullity. These things are actually incapacitating defects which render a person incapable of entering into a valid marriage. Homosexuality is, of course, a more dramatic example, but the cause of the invalidity is basically the same: The person is not capable of sustaining the burdens and obligations of marriage.

Isn't all this changing in the law somewhat discouraging? I mean everything seems to be up for grabs. How do you answer those who see this kind of thinking as merely the beginning of a general moral breakdown in the church?

Times are changing. God's law is unchanging, but men often make God's law appear narrower and more severe than it really is. If the supreme law is charity, then it is charity that must pervade the interpretation of all law. Justice tempered with mercy is the very meaning of canonical equity, which is a judicious application of the general law to a particular human situation. In many of these matters, the faithful are already presuming to act on the basis of their conscience, because their own sense of justice has been outraged; and they are not to be blamed. In a legal system where many tribunals are capable of holding up human lives for years and years while an apparently half-hearted investigation is carried on, we are in no position to criticize. Some of these people may very well be subjectively deluded, but others have asked the church for bread and have been handed a stone. The issue is one of justice.

The law is designed to serve the common good, but the mission of Christ was to save individuals. We must find the balance. In the words of Ivo of Chartres (c. 1040-1116 A.D.): "We urge the prudent reader, when judging the merit of contrary texts, to keep before his eyes the end of law, which is the salvation of souls, and the fact that some things are said in a spirit of moderation and mercy."

So you're saying that the reason more church annulments are being granted these days is not because of a growing laxity on the part of the tribunals, but because of greater fidelity to human rights by church jurists.

Yes, beautifully put. Remember, however, that expediency does not transcend the moral law. The issue as I mentioned is one of justice and it is a justice tempered with mercy that should be distinguished in Christ's church. It is not a matter of giving everyone what they think is their right. It is a matter of giving everyone what is their just due, no more, no less.

3. Pastoral Possibilities Where Annulments Are Not Possible

Why has it been so difficult in the past to obtain an annulment in the church?

In the past, and to a lesser extent in the present, innumerable persons deserving of marriage annulments were unable to obtain one for reasons that are all too human. Sometimes the parish priest was at fault, advising a man that he had no case when in fact he did.

Often the tribunal's heavy case load was the culprit. Those cases which reached some tribunals may never be completed because of inefficiency or poor organization due to understaffing.

Then there is the problem of processing the case. Some petitions based on solid grounds for an annulment have never been completed because the key witnesses refused to cooperate. There is also the problem of human fallibility on the part of the judges. In some instances cases have been tried and annulments denied because the judges involved based their decisions on an overly strict notion of the moral certitude required of them. These weaknesses are still operative and neither the experimental procedural norms nor the zeal of many dedicated priests working in our tribunals can erase them.

What can be done for these people?

The central issue in this whole problem of caring for these people is not with the tribunal itself or, for that matter, with canon law which regulates tribunal practice. And it is not with the recent norms issued by Rome to placate the protest arising from all corners of the American church. The central issue is the bishop's awareness of his role in the Christian community. The question is an ecclesiological one: Is each bishop providing adequate pastoral care for those in his diocese who have suffered the tragedy of a broken marriage? There is much more to pastoral care than merely setting up a tribunal.

The Constitution on the Church, Section 27, of the Second Vatican Council states: "Bishops govern the particular churches entrusted to them as the vicars and ambassadors of Christ. . . . This power, which they personally exercise in Christ's name, is proper, ordinary and immediate, although its exercise is ultimately regulated by the supreme authority of the church and can be circumscribed by certain limits for the advantage of the church of the faithful. In virtue of this power *bishops have the sacred right and the duty before the Lord to make laws for their subjects, to pass judgment on them, and to moderate everything pertaining to the ordering of worship and the apostolate.*"

On the local level we are sorely in need of courageous pastoral remedies to these exceptional cases, especially when we realize that for the past few decades so few annulment cases were actually processed in this country. As recently as 1969, 57 out of 153 tribunals in the United States did not even render one formal decision in a year. Twenty-three published only one decision and nine gave two decisions. Fortunately, this situation has changed drastically for the better, but there is still a problem. The bishop's role is decisive in the matter of leadership in showing concern for people with marriage problems.

Specifically, can you tell me about the "internal forum solution," or the good-conscience marriage?

The internal forum solution has been used as a safety valve for the inadequacies of our tribunals. In the United States, hundreds of deserving couples have been readmitted to the sacraments, even though their present marriage was never technically revalidated in the church. In the past Catholics were led to believe that the reward of heaven or the pain of hell was somehow related to the judgment of canon lawyers, but this is an incorrect understanding of revelation. A person's destiny before God is not necessarily based on his juridical standing in the Catholic Church. Those who thought this way are changing and the younger people, generally, will have none of it. Very few Catholics under the age of 25 suffer from scruples in this regard, but countless Catholics have been formed in a different mold and they still endure much unnecessary suffering. Even those who have received an "internal forum solution" to their problem and have been permitted to receive the sacraments still long for the day when their reputation and state of life will be entirely vindicated by the church. They look to the official church for some remedy to their marital situation, and they should have it.

Could you be more specific? How does it work?

This will take a little time to develop, but let me use a particular case as an example. Let us suppose that a girl was abandoned by her husband within a year or so of their marriage. He left, telling her that he only married her to give the baby a name and that he never intended to stay with her permanently. She would have solid grounds for an ecclesiastic annulment case. It would then be her burden to prove these facts in an ecclesiastical court. Technically she should present two or more witnesses to establish conclusively that her husband lied to the priest before the marriage when he was asked: "Do you intend a permanent union?" It must be remembered that if it was a Catholic marriage the parish church most probably has the husband's signature on a sworn document stating, among other things, that he did intend a permanent union.

The difficult burden of proving that he lied at the time of the marriage falls on her. Because this is so difficult, only a percentage of the petitions presented to the church court in the past had hope of arriving at a completely successful decision. So where does this girl stand? Her husband has deceived her, but she is not able to produce the necessary evidence to convince the church officials of the invalidity of her marriage. Today a creative canonist might accept her testimony as true or work the case on other grounds, but years ago it would have been abandoned. Even today, however, in some places, that girl would have no chance for an annulment.

What procedures would she have to go through in the tribunal if they did hear the case? And what would she do if she lost in the tribunal?

The church officials would, of course, ask her many questions. How do you know he lied when he married you? How can we be sure he didn't marry you with a correct intention but only changed afterwards? How can we be convinced that his intention, prior to marriage, actually influenced his consent on the day of your wedding?

And the girl may find herself only able to say: "I just know he didn't intend to stay with me, I just know it." She can find no witnesses; she can offer no legal proof. Once it becomes clear that she cannot prove her allegation, some church officials might be satisfied that they did all they could, and drop the case. The girl finds herself stranded at a very young age to the frightening alternatives of living alone for the rest of her life, or of marrying again outside the church. She wants neither.

Let us suppose she meets someone else, falls in love and marries him before a justice of the peace. What happens to her Catholicity? Not too long ago the law was clear on this point. When a Catholic divorced and remarried a Catholic outside the church, both parties to the second marriage were excommunicated. Fortunately this penalty has been lifted retroactively by the American hierarchy, the same body that imposed it. Nevertheless, she and her new husband are both considered to be invalidly and, therefore, sinfully married because her first marriage is considered valid.

This example of a second marriage which appears to be invalid can be referred to as a good-conscience marriage. It is valid before God, but technically invalid before the church. In such a case, two serious questions arise: (1) is it possible for the parties of such a marriage to consider themselves true members of the church; and (2) under the circumstances, would they ever be able to receive the Eucharist? Such questions cannot be answered for people in a general way. Each case must be weighed individually. Nevertheless, certain general observations can be made to clarify the issue.

We are certain that a person is made a member of the church through baptism, and by this sacrament the right is given to receive all the other sacraments. If a woman is certain that she was defrauded in such a way that her first marriage was no marriage in the true sense, it is difficult to see why her second marriage should separate her and her new spouse from God and from the Eucharistic community. The real problem arises in connection with the desire of the people to be reconciled openly with the Catholic community. Under the present law of the church, if she cannot produce solid evidence in court, there is no canonical solution. However, for the sake of peace of conscience such a couple is not without some remedy. Her conscience, and his, will have to guide them.

How could the second marriage be valid if a priest could not marry them?

Naturally a priest would not be permitted to marry someone who has been previously married and who has not had that marriage annulled. Canon 1098 of the Code of Canon Law, however, might offer some relief. This canon states: "If it is impossible, without grave inconvenience, to send for or go to a pastor or Ordinary, or a priest delegated by either of these to assist at a marriage, another priest who can come should be called upon and he should assist at the marriage together with witnesses *but the marriage would be valid in the presence of the witnesses alone.*"

Here we are describing a situation, where, because of grave inconvenience no priest is "available" to perform the marriage rite. The classic example would be the case of the man and a woman alone on an island. There is no priest available, but the two parties are free to marry, and they want to marry. In such a case they merely exchange consent and confer the sacrament on each other. In a less dramatic setting, if a priest was not available the marriage "would be valid in the presence of the witnesses alone." Therefore, couples who marry before a legally qualified official and two witnesses, because no priest can marry them, have a good argument in this canon to justify their belief that they have enjoyed a valid reception of the sacrament of Matrimony. The essence of the sacrament is the exchange of consent; the two parties always confer the sacrament on each other.

In such a case can the parties begin to receive Holy Communion?

Yes. When a person is inwardly well disposed to receive and is not living in sin, but is prevented from receiving more because of legal formalism than true justice, it is reasonable to assume that Holy Communion may be received provided no scandal be given in such an act. Obviously, scandal must be avoided at all costs, or the sacrament would be dishonored. But if scandal can be avoided individuals have every right to exercise their conscience and to unite themselves with the Lord by the reception of his most sacred body and blood.

A priest should be consulted in the privacy of the confessional. The priest in this matter is a judge in the tribunal of mercy and he can exercise his function for the church by assisting the penitent to form a good conscience according to the circumstances of the case presented to him. This merely transfers the question from the external forum to the internal forum of the confessional. The priest can reassure the penitent that in delicate matters such as these the private conscience can be trusted.

Have there been any official permissions for this from the hierarchy?

The Dutch Catechism is a refreshing breeze in this whole aspect of marriage. The bishops of Holland had this to say in matters involving a conflict between a just law and the personal conscience: "In such cases, a thorough discussion with a prudent spiritual director can free a person from much unnecessary fear. It can even happen that a believer comes to the conclusion that his marriage does not bind him in conscience." That's a rather enlightened statement, but we have not as yet heard anything as forthright from our own hierarchy.

Several years ago there was a discussion in the Catholic press concerning the issue of the internal forum, and some negative statements were made by Rome concerning a procedure that had been adopted. Could you describe and clarify what happened in that situation?

I think there was a misunderstanding of the whole issue. The internal forum refers to the person's conscience in relation to God. You are referring to an action which reversed a new custom being practiced in tribunals. What happened was this — a few bishops developed procedures in their dioceses for granting official permission for individuals with good conscience to return to the sacraments, in cases where an annulment could not be proved. For some time individual priests had been allowing people to return to the sacraments in an unofficial way. But these bishops established norms for granting such permission in the open. They wanted to regularize what they thought had become a subjective decision on the part of those who were counseling couples. It was a sincere pastoral effort to bring peace of soul to many deserving people.

But it was the public nature of the procedure that Rome objected to?

Yes. The validity of the forum of conscience was not at issue. That's a matter of moral and sacramental theology, not canon law. What Rome objected to, as I see it, was the trend of bishops who were making local laws, which means bringing to the external forum a new procedure which contradicted traditional tribunal practice. The church always reserves the right to declare marriages invalid, but only the supreme lawmaker, the pope, can make the laws. The principle of indissolubility was not the issue.

The letter that came from Rome which Cardinal Krol, acting in his capacity as president of the American hierarchy at the time, sent to all the bishops, stated that this trend was not to continue. Very soon afterwards the bishops who had begun the practice stopped it. It appeared as if they had been ordered to do so by Rome. But my impression was that no bishop was reprimanded, only the future extension of the practice was prohibited. You see, Rome didn't want a new public law or custom developing which would put aside the procedural laws of the Code. This has nothing to do with what happens in the confessional, or in the private thoughts of an individual. No priests were contacted or forbidden to absolve in these complex cases.

You were the chief judge for 10 years in a diocesan marriage court. If a person was unable to get a declaration of nullity in the court procedures, yet in good conscience did not consider his second marriage to be a sinful union, would you feel justified in advising him that he could receive the sacraments?

It would depend on the reasons why he did not receive the annulment. If he had good reason to suspect the validity of the first marriage, I believe I would have a moral

duty to support his conscience and reconcile him with
Christ.

**In fact there are a good number of church leaders who are
very cautious about this and try to dissuade priests from this
practice. You are aware of this?**

Caution is rightly urged by the authorities, because I
have personally witnessed abuses which were indefensible.
I have seen priests disregard every law, even to having a
public Mass to bless a marriage that is canonically irregular,
implying to the general public that this is all canonically
proper. Pastors, too, are rightly concerned about these
abuses. But we cannot ignore deserving couples, and we
must respect the conscience of these good people.

I think that procedures will vary from place to place,
because of the possibility of scandal. It has been my
practice, in helping people to resolve their consciences and
return to the sacraments, always to talk to the local pastor
about the issue of scandal. Usually it is the case that no one
in the parish knows about the former marriage, but it is still
best to talk to the local pastor. Even among the most
conservative pastors I have found an openness to this
solution.

**A different situation — what about a person in a second
marriage which can never be recognized by the church
because the first marriage was undoubtedly valid? What
pastoral support can be given to a person in that situation?**

As you present it, that is a less flexible situation than the
ones we have been talking about. My sympathies go out to a
person in that situation; there are some people we just can't
help. But my experience with broken marriages tells me that
we should not automatically assume that the first marriage
was a valid one. I would try to dig a little deeper. Many

times people are convinced that their first marriage was valid because of the external evidence — they were married before a priest and there was a reception and a honeymoon. It all might look very matter-of-fact. But, from a legal point of view, I don't think we can always assume that it was valid, without taking the time to investigate it.

I would say that Christ gave us a clear example of what our attitude should be when he met the Samaritan woman at the well. His actions should indicate what his intention was. He not only spoke to her, a Samaritan—which was forbidden by Jewish law—but he sent her on a mission for him. She was the first to announce the Messiah to non-Jews. He commissioned her after telling her that she wasn't truly married and was living with her sixth husband. This doesn't look like a merciless legal stance. It looks more like an acceptance of the person.

Likewise, if we look on people in similar circumstances as wretched sinners and close the door in their faces, then I would say that we have not understood the mind of Christ. We should meet them with a spirit of mercy and under-standing and tolerance, with reassurance that God's love is not cut off from anyone, especially someone who is genuinely trying to turn to him. I try to offer them consolation and encouragement.

What about the person who wants more than consolation? The person who wants to return to the sacraments?

That is a very difficult situation. The presumption of the validity of the first marriage may be wrong. I would ask first of all: Do you feel that you're living in sin? Do you understand your present marriage to be an adulterous union? If the person has responsibly studied the statements of the church, thoughtfully reviewed his life situation with a priest, if he has struggled with the delicate and difficult questions that are involved and still has no sense of sin, then he ought not be deprived of the Eucharist. The benefit of the doubt should favor the human conscience.

This is often argued the other way.

I realize that. But in order for the force of law to be binding, it must take root in conscience. The Vatican II Document on Religious Freedom has stated the overall importance of conscience in the attribution of sin, and we have a responsibility to look upon the consciences of such people with respect. As you explore a human conscience, and find it deeply rooted in responsible certainty, with no sense of being in sin, then that conscience must be respected. On this level, the issue becomes the issue of conscience, not the issue of indissolubility. The principle of indissolubility remains, and I do not expect the church to change its stance on that principle. But the sober, well-informed and responsible conscience must be respected.

Then you are saying that the only internal forum obstacle to the reception of the Eucharist is a bad conscience — the persons believe that they are living in a sinful way that alienates them from Christ. A confessor, after testing a conscience seriously and objectively, can only take the individuals at their word and, if there is no sense of sin, admit them to the sacraments; or, if there is a sense of sin, deny them.

The conscience has to be respected, even if the priest disagrees with its conclusions. There is no ecclesiastical, papal or divine precept that says we *must* accuse someone of mortal sin. In this matter of internal forum, or conscience solution, I feel the church in its structures and laws is doing its best to witness to the person and teaching of Christ. We haven't witnessed to the mercy of Christ well enough in the past. As a result, many people have been rejected by the church and have never come back.

And many of them confronted humanly impossible obstacles in their attempts to find a solution to their bad marriage situations within the church.

Yes, and there is still a prejudice against the efficiency of the tribunal system because of this. Past injustices have created a deep suspicion in this area. Today, however, I think there is a very good likelihood the cases can be tried and receive affirmative decisions. I believe the effort should be made, and I would disagree with those who might just want to take the easy way out by going to their pastor and asking for readmittance to the sacraments on the basis of their good conscience.

Would most parish priests have enough experience to advise a couple about the usefulness of submitting a case? Should a couple look around for a priest who is well informed about present procedures?

Right now the process is very simple. It's just a matter of getting in touch with someone who is on the tribunal. Most of them will be able to handle skillfully the cases that are brought to them. If a particular tribunal has the reputation for being quite conservative, then it would be wise to avoid it.

Do you foresee any major developments in canonical thought on these issues in the next five years?

I think the evolution will continue. Jurisprudence is still developing even within the Roman Rota. This evolution will increase the grounds on which marriages may be declared invalid. I think it is unfortunately true that many Catholics and non-Catholics will have the false impression that we are in effect becoming less strict and granting what amounts to Catholic divorces. People will have that impression even though the church will continue to uphold its position on indissolubility. But this radical change in the criteria for valid marriages will give us a better and more merciful way of approaching people in bad marriage situations. Perhaps the juridical, legal patterns we use now will be replaced. We will probably move in the direction of a more pastoral quasi-judicial procedure. In other words we will move away from a court procedure.

As a man who respects the work of the courts, how would you answer the criticism that the judges are only playing games? It sometimes appears that if you dig hard enough you can always find some basis for nullity in any marriage.

We're dealing with human lives. My only concern is that we render justice. Expanding the grounds for annulment, simplifying our procedures to grant justice more speedily — if these reforms look like playing games, then I think people have the wrong impression. We want to take as compassionate a stand as possible within the system. Maybe the church in the future will find some other way to deal with these situations. Right now I think we are doing the best we can with what we have. Remember there are negative decisions being rendered, so not every petition ends in an annulment.

A final question on this topic. Are there any historical patterns in our ecclesiastical experience that relate to the efforts of the marriage courts to be more compassionate?

Yes. Excluding the Greek Church's belief that a marriage can die and be no longer binding, and the Protestant ethic which is basically the same thing, there are some historical precedents in our own Catholic faith. In Celtic penitential books of the fifth, sixth and seventh centuries we find reference to the principle of *oeconomia,* which was a way of tempering the harsh impact of the law applied strictly as law. In Europe and Asia Minor there were practices by bishops which resolved these same pastoral problems in ways that differ only slightly from modern developments.

For example, one woman was the wife of a sailor and mother of five children. Her husband went off to sea and decided to abandon his wife and family. He never returned with his ship. After living alone for a long time and having no means of supporting herself, she went to the bishop because another man had asked her to marry. She asked the bishop what she was to do, since her first marriage was valid and indissoluble. The bishop, using the principle of *oeconomia,* said, "Let her remarry." Other bishops did the same thing. Confronting human weakness, the church permitted what traditional thinkers would consider to be theologically improper.

In our own century, 40 or 50 years ago, the bishops of Chicago were facing the problem of converting the black families in the diocese. Parents of black children in the parochial schools approached the parishes asking to become Catholic. The pastors had to turn them away time and again because many of them were found to be in a second or even third marriage. Legally, they couldn't be accepted into the church.

"What can we do?" the pastors asked. The hierarchy made a simple pastoral judgment. They decided, from then on, to allow these parents to be admitted into the church. Thenceforth, the "marriage in possession" would be considered the valid one. Canonically this was illogical. But on a pastoral level they made a decision based on mercy, understanding and compassion. In my judgment they were right, because most of these earlier marriages could have been annulled in an ecclesiastical court today anyway.

In a similar way, those who are now involved in the tribunal system are trying to witness to the mercy of the Lord as well as to the indissolubility of marriage.

4. The Future of Ecclesiastical Tribunals

What, in your opinion, is the shape of things to come?

You mean regarding the tribunal system?

Yes.

That sounds like a simple question but it isn't. The central issue is the doctrine of the church on indissolubility. In this country the divorce mentality has begun to erode confidence in the attainability of a permanent marriage. People ask how the bond can be considered indissoluble when it can be broken so easily? But the Gospels call men and women to a permanent commitment in marriage. The church gives witness to this belief in her laws. The future isn't going to change human nature and gospel values. Adultery is still going to be adultery. The same questions will be asked 400 years from now: Who is married to whom? Is this a true marriage? Does this union bind for life? Since the questions haven't changed in 2,000 years, they certainly won't change in the next 400 years.

Yes, but won't the answers change?

I think the methods for finding the answers will undoubtedly change. What seems to be happening now is that we are slower to presume we have the final answer. We're more willing to admit we're dealing with mystery.

Could you expand on that a little?

Well, if you look at the evolution in the church tribunals which took place between 1967 and 1977, you'll see some amazing changes. The same basic legal structure, the Code of Canon Law, produced astonishingly different results over the years.

While I was the chief judge of the Paterson tribunal in the mid-60s and early 70s, the case flow throughout the country was increasing from a trickle to a heavy flow. At that time some tribunals were very conservative and they actually denied the petitioners their right to have their case tried in a church court. I wrote an article in *Commonweal* in 1967 entitled, "The Church and Second Marriage," encouraging the laity to exercise their consciences when they received unfair treatment from the church courts. A person has a natural right to marry and sometimes that right is still intact even though a marriage ceremony once took place.

I have been amazed at the evolution which has occurred since I wrote that piece. The new norms have loosened up the whole system so that rights are being vindicated and justice being served more and more.

What do you think will be the method for handling these cases in future years?

I think the tribunal system will still function because people do want clear-cut answers. They will need legal solutions to the tangle of human relationships. But the legalistic approach will be lessened. It's one thing to have fair laws; it's another thing entirely to have legalistic judges. However, I think the bypassing of church tribunals will increase. Priests will continue to offer communion to anyone disposed in conscience to receive it.

Eventually, I think we will have a simple fact-finding system presided over by a pastoral panel. The panel will give permission for a couple to marry based on the doubt of the validity of the first marriage. It will not be an annulment per se; it will be a presumption of freedom urged for pastoral considerations. The new marriage will then be given the presumption of validity.

While this procedure will resolve many cases, there will still be a tribunal system to grant ecclesiastical annulments for the more complicated cases referred to it by the pastoral panel.

Do you think Catholics in the year 2025 will care that much about following any tribunal procedure?

There will always be people who believe in the gospel of Jesus Christ and who will trust the wisdom of the church. They will want to do the right thing, and they will follow the guidance of the church in this matter.

Why does there have to be so much pain and controversy in all this if we're going to end up pretty much like the Anglicans anyway?

I don't know if you have it quite right. The church is trying to stand against the corroding influence of secularism which does not regard the marriage vows as binding. Today, expediency and convenience are the norm. The church has been courageous in holding out against these attitudes and she will continue to do so. What is changing, however, is the fact that an exclusively legalistic approach is no longer adequate to deal with the sheer volume of cases.

Isn't this expediency?

It is surely an accommodation, but it is not a change of principle. The church must maintain her fidelity to the gospel but the message is not always understood in exactly the same way in different centuries. We know a great deal more now about the meaning of Christ's words than we did 100 years ago.

Wouldn't it be a reasonable thing for a critic of the church to say the church has become more lax and just won't admit it?

I think we have become more fair, not more lax. Some cases lasted more than 10 years in the courts. Many deserving cases never got a hearing. The moral certainty required before a judge could grant an affirmative decision was so strict that it seemed to go beyond right reason. Moving away from those abuses does not mean we've become more lax in the real sense of the word.

It is not unlike the development of scripture exegesis. For centuries Catholics were required to take the bible literally, but now, in a text like that of Jonah, we no longer feel it necessary to believe he was actually in the belly of a whale for three days. The literal interpretation is unacceptable today. When people first departed from that position they were considered laxists, and even heretics. So the accusations are not new. They just sound new. Change always produces anxiety and very often that anxiety is expressed in terms of danger. I can assure you a more humane and a more just system is not dangerous.

One last question. How do you counsel or comfort those who have been wounded by churchmen in some way, because of the way they were treated?

There is always grace, so I think some answer might be possible. It's a tough question. I am reminded of the woman whom I call the patron saint of victims of the Catholic tribunal system. Her name is Joan of Arc. She was condemned to be burned at the stake by a church tribunal, and she was innocent. Some people may take comfort in the fact that the church does eventually get around to justice. Her condemnation was lifted and the decision of her judges was eventually reversed. It made a great saint of Joan, but I think we could have been a bit more humble about the magnitude of the error of our learned jurists. Nevertheless, Joan was undaunted. Among her last words is recorded what I consider the greatest human act of forgiveness. I can only lift them up to be seen and judged by the wounded of this century. Joan said, "I love the church, I will always love the church, because for me the church is Jesus Christ."